New Solos
for Classical Mandolin

Concert Repertoire for Practice & Performance

BY AUGUST WATTERS

illustrations by Alex Timmerman

ISBN 978-1-5400-4805-9

Visit Hal Leonard Online at
www.halleonard.com

Contact us:
Hal Leonard
7777 West Bluemound Road
Milwaukee, WI 53213
Email: info@halleonard.com

In Europe, contact:
Hal Leonard Europe Limited
42 Wigmore Street
Marylebone, London, W1U 2RN
Email: info@halleonardeurope.com

In Australia, contact:
Hal Leonard Australia Pty. Ltd.
4 Lentara Court
Cheltenham, Victoria, 3192 Australia
Email: info@halleonard.com.au

Giuseppi Tartini
Basilica of Saint Anthony
Padua, Italy

This book is dedicated to my teachers, especially three who helped me to become a composing music teacher:

David Baker
William G. Leavitt
Hal Crook

Each had an uncanny ability to compose classroom examples that were also satisfying as musical compositions. By setting a high standard for music designed to teach, as well as to inspire, these artists modeled ways to cultivate composition and teaching as two symbiotic aspects of a professional career in music. May their musical traditions live on.

Table of Contents

Acknowledgments

Many thanks to those who helped me through this project with feedback, encouragement, advice, and other suggestions. My proofreaders were essential in helping to understand what needed more explanation. I also received some indispensable advice from other teachers. I hope all of our efforts have made this book more useful to the next generation of creative mandolinists.

My most sincere thanks to:

> Salima Ben Guigui
> Eugene Braig
> Jean Comeau
> John Craton
> Julane Deener
> John McClain
> Michael Reichenbach
> Paul Ruppa
> Joe Thomas
> Alex Timmerman
> Adam Us

I never met Joe Carr, but am happy to dedicate a tune to him in this book. Joe wrote good teaching materials for mandolin, and was at the center of America's first college program to include mandolinists, at South Plains College, in Texas. It's only a matter of time (I hope!) before the American classical mandolin finds an academic home.

A warm thanks to Salvatore Mancino, Emanuele Cappellotto, and the members of the MandolinVenice ensemble, who have made my own learning experiences in Italy so much deeper.

A special thanks to historian Paul Ruppa, who has shined a light on early chapters of the American mandolin. And thanks to Sheri Mignano Crawford and John T. La Barbera, who have worked to document and present Italian mandolin music in its transition to North America, as well as its influence on what followed. Without these early developments, today's American mandolin music would be unimaginable.

And of course, thanks to my wife Nancy, as we continue to build our lives and successes around the most improbable combination of interests.

Foreword: State of the Craft

Compositions, transcriptions, and *arrangements* are all part of classical mandolin music today. But there's a difference between classical mandolin music, and classical music on mandolin.

Some mandolinists prefer music composed for mandolin: from this perspective, focusing on music built around the characteristic strengths and weaknesses of our instrument gives us easiest access to the widest expressive range. Classical mandolin, after all, is an expression of classical music: a form that engages us in a timeless dialogue across generations; a conversation about how to communicate human emotion through its most articulate language: music. By opening ourselves to what others have discovered on this path, we become fully empowered to develop our own expressive voice.

Then again, there are other perspectives! Transcribing familiar music from other instruments to mandolin offers an immediate and satisfying way to explore classical music. It's also a creative process that is well-represented within our own mandolin traditions, and for good reason: there's no better way, than a familiar melody, to connect to an audience! Works transcribed from other instruments (such as the violin works of J.S. Bach) have become a major entry point for mandolinists to "classical music on mandolin."

Taking the idea of transcriptions a step farther, some mandolinists treat classical music mainly as source material for new arrangements. We've all heard accomplished mandolinists who have adapted classical works, re-orchestrating and re-harmonizing at will. Today's easy access to classical compositions seems an endless source for those with the familiarity, sensitivity, and skill (!!) required. You might say, in fact, that arrangements close the circle back to composition: a skilled mandolin arranger is really a specialized type of composer who adapts music borrowed from a different instrument, taking advantage of the idiomatic techniques of mandolin.

New Solos for Classical Mandolin is built around my view that all three tools—composition, transcription, and arranging—are valuable. These new solos, composed for mandolin, are based on right-hand techniques borrowed from the literature of the classical mandolin. There are also exercises to further develop these techniques, along with studies designed to build your fluency with the underlying language of scales, arpeggios, chords, and harmonic progressions. The conceptual and instrumental skills targeted here will be useful later on, in composition, arranging, and improvisation.

I have not attempted to explain the underlying musical theory, since that information is readily available and beyond the scope of this collection. To get the most from this book, you may wish to turn to other sources for further study of its musical language. Or, you may choose just to focus on the solos, and learn by example.

I hope that this book will help you, whatever your musical background or interests, to enjoy and participate in music-making. Enjoy!

Roots of the American Mandolin

It has been several years since Berklee Press approached me with the idea that classical mandolin should be represented in their catalogue, since it has a lively presence in today's music industry. Classical mandolin has continued to grow into a significant area of interest among American mandolinists, especially as new discoveries and publications bring the classical roots of the American mandolin more clearly into focus. More than ever, our classical mandolin traditions offer players at all levels an interesting and rewarding way to explore the instrument, and to connect with other musicians. For professionals, it offers potential career paths in community music. For the next generation of serious musicians, understanding this foundational chapter of the American mandolin is essential not only to forming an international perspective, but also to fully appreciating our instrument's future possibilities.

Introduction

Welcome! to this new collection exploring some possibilities of the solo classical mandolin. Although the solos are not composed in a "classical" style, they draw heavily on classical mandolin techniques. I hope you enjoy them for practice or performance, and they lead you to other music composed for mandolin. There are as many ways to interpret these solos as there are mandolinists, so there can be no definitive version.

Classical mandolin should not be just about historical styles, or music transposed from another instrument! The music in this book is designed to help you explore the textural possibilities of mandolin, while also developing your technique and practice method. Most of the solos are accompanied by exercises, each delving deeper into the right-hand techniques presented: Alternate picking, rest strokes, consecutive downstrokes, reverse alternate picking, and glide strokes.

My previous book *Exploring Classical Mandolin* (Berklee Press, 2015) describes these techniques in detail and includes easy original etudes for practice. *New Solos for Classical Mandolin* builds on that framework, beginning at a basic level and expanding from there. Instead of discussing these ideas, *New Solos* takes a by-example approach, with a minimum of explanation. The techniques are introduced gradually, so that each section depends on understanding the previous. As you progress, you'll find opportunities in the earlier sections to apply what comes later: Once you get some practice with glide strokes (introduced in Section III), for example, you'll find places to apply them in Section I as well (where they are marked as optional).

A Layered Approach
Since this book is designed for mandolinists at different levels of experience, you will find a variety of challenges at different levels within each section. The basic skill set needed is moderate facility getting around the fingerboard, and ability to read standard notation. It is not necessary to complete one section before going on to the next, although I do recommend focusing primarily on one technique at a time. Section Four requires familiarity with all the previous materials, and Section Five presents more advanced technical challenges. If something is not clear to you, move on to the next piece, and circle back later. Gradually, the new ideas will filter in, as you find them repeated in different ways.

Exercises: Making Them Your Own
As you progress, you'll notice that each exercise page further explores the technical and musical challenges of its corresponding solo. The "Development" pages extend the content of each section's exercises, followed by topics not often included in classical mandolin methods: chord vocabulary, chord/melody relationships, and voice leading of both chords and arpeggios. In my view, these are essential tools for the classical mandolinist, since a deeper understanding of the musical language makes easier work of reading and memorization. You'll also find those skills are helpful with improvisation, arranging, and composition.

One of the most valuable skills this book can help you develop is learning to analyze a new piece you're studying, and invent your own exercises to address its technical challenges. Always be looking for ways to synthesize what you're learning with what you already know. For example, the minor scales in Development 2 can be combined with the scale patterns in Development 1, just as the major scales in Development 1 should also be explored with the more challenging scale patterns of Development 2. The "Exercises for 'Gliding Home'" introduce G minor arpeggios—this would be a good time to plug those G minor arpeggios into the previous arpeggio patterns. And always remember to transpose—by ear—to new keys!

Picking conventions
Alternate picking (picking down on the beat and up off the beat) is a convention that occurs in many musical genres, including classical mandolin. Often alternate picking leads to different fingering choices than would a downstroke approach (where shifting to a new course requires a downstroke) or a glide stroke approach (two or more consecutive pick strokes in the same direction); yet these techniques often coexist. (For example: in measure 24 of "Scottish Bells," the indicated fingering matches the indicated down-up picking pattern, not the optional glide stroke.)

We begin with alternate picking and rest strokes (a form of downstroke where the pick comes to rest on the adjacent course), followed by a gradual introduction of the downstroke approach. Other techniques drawn from the classical literature, such as reverse alternate picking and glide strokes, follow.

The palm mute, introduced in the "Exercises for 'Scottish Bells'," is intended to stop one course (or more) from sounding while picking notes on a higher (closer to the floor) course. In measure 7, beat 3 of "Scottish Bells," the right hand should mute the open G while picking the G an octave higher. The palm mute is one way to control unwanted resonances. With practice, picking and muting can be done in one motion.

The Downstroke Approach to Picking
With a few exceptions (such as arpeggios), I usually move from one course to the next using a downstroke. This "downstroke approach" helps to unify the sound of the melodic line by minimizing timbral changes between courses, and between upstroke and downstroke. Alternate picking and consecutive downstrokes are both components of this approach, so it is important to internalize the sensation of those techniques first.

When should a downstroke also be a rest stroke? Myron Bickford, one of North America's most influential mandolin and guitar teachers, recommended that the downstroke should always end by resting the pick on the next higher string (or on the instrument's top, in the case of the E string). I find that to be good advice, and usually workable.

Fingering Conventions
Normally (in first position) the first finger covers frets 1 and 2, the second finger covers frets 3 and 4, third on 5 and 6, and the fourth finger is on fret 7. Written-in fingerings usually indicate an exception to the rule. These exceptions may improve ease of fingering or add expression (for example, in measure 4 of "Scottish Bells," fingering C with the second finger makes it easier to sustain the A at the beginning of the measure).

Double-stops and chords may also use different fingerings at different times to facilitate what comes before or after. I'm sure you'll find ways to improve fingering that work best for you, but I advise following the written fingerings first, to be sure you understand their logic. Never hesitate to omit notes when necessary, for the sake of playability—you can always add them later, as your fingers adapt. If chord fingerings seem unclear, remember the usual fingering conventions!

Finding a natural left-hand position for chords, and avoiding uncomfortable stretches, often requires exceptions to the usual left-hand fingerings. For chord playing, the left hand often falls into a somewhat more collapsed, comfortable shape, spanning only two or three frets between first and fourth fingers.

Position Playing
To organize the playing positions higher up the neck (when your first finger moves above the second fret), classical mandolin methods often use a system of position playing identical to violin. This book does not explore position playing thoroughly, but does include a basic introduction to the second and third positions. In these cases, position shifts are indicated by fingering, as well as roman numerals in italics. Half position (first finger covers fret 1 only) is also introduced.

Open Strings
We often choose whether to play E, A, or D on the open string or on the seventh fret of the adjacent string. In this book, any note available on an open string should be played open, unless otherwise indicated. Occasionally, the "0" indication is added for extra clarity. In classical mandolin we tend to use the closed fingerings more often, and this is indicated by a written-in fingering. When playing above first position, those same E, A, and D notes normally do not have indicated fingerings (even though they're played closed), since they follow the higher position fingerings.

The choice of when to use an open string is also related to your choice of picking technique. Since Section One begins with alternate picking, it's safe to say that you'll approach those early scale exercises differently later on, once you are ready to incorporate other picking techniques.

Phrase Markings

In this book, phrase markings indicate that the notes should be played legato and allowed to sustain together when possible. Sometimes alternative fingerings help to facilitate: In measure 12 of "The Story of the Rest," playing the E with the second finger allows that note to sustain while the first finger plays the G#. In measure 21, the pairing of fingers 1 and 3 (Bb-G) and 2 and 4 (B-G#) keeps the hand in a more natural position as those two pairs of double-stops sustain.

Learning by Ear

Rather than writing out scale and arpeggio exercises completely, I often include just enough to establish a pattern—your ear will tell you what comes next! "Etc." means "continue the pattern by ear." Scales and arpeggios should be learned primarily this way, to build the ear-to-finger associations and muscle memory we use when reading music or improvising. In the "Exercises for 'The Story of the Rest,'" Exercise One contains five versions of a four-measure scale pattern, with each repetition changing one note. Exercise Two uses the same five statements, although only three are written out—the last two you'll find by ear, once your ear recognizes the pattern. Exercise Three also uses the same five statements, but only the first is written.

Arpeggio Method

Most classical mandolin methods present arpeggios as primarily a technical exercise. I prefer to practice arpeggios in a way that is closer to their musical function, i.e., by placing them in context of a chord progression, where they usually follow familiar patterns. You will see that there are just a few easily memorized formulas, and that mastering them is really a matter of making the ear-to-finger connection for what your ear already intuitively knows.

Chord/Melody Relationships

Since "chord-melody" is often understood as a jazz conception rather than an essential part of a classical mandolin method, I will add a word about its place in classical mandolin traditions: a working knowledge of chords—and how to connect one to the next, so that the linear motion between the highest note of two successive chord voicings is perceived as a melody—was an integral part of some historical mandolin methods (see Appendix II). Today, this "chord-melody" concept is as useful as ever, since internalizing common melodic connections between chords makes those patterns, as they occur in the music, easier to recognize. The payoff comes in sight-reading, memorization, and composition.

"Chord-melody," as I have defined it, is exactly the same concept as in the jazz world. There are, however, two differences in my presentation: first, the chord-melody method presented here is triadic (except for the V7 chord), rather than being applied to four-note chords. Further, jazz chord-melody on mandolin is most often approached as one melody note voiced above two chord tones (usually the third and seventh). I prefer to structure a mandolin chord-melody method as I learned long ago, from my jazz guitar teachers: by simply memorizing three inversions for each triad, and four for each seventh chord.

Building Sets for Performance

For performance, you might choose to arrange two or three solos into a set. No doubt you'll find moods and colors, hidden within the phrases, that are all your own. Classical mandolin is a living tradition! I hope that this book will help you to enjoy your journey, and to make your own personal contribution.

August Watters
March, 2019

Part I: Downstrokes, Rest Strokes, and Alternate Picking

Scottish Bells

downstrokes and alternate picking, optional glide strokes

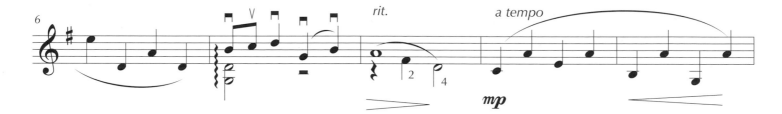

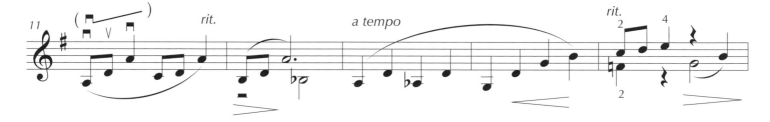

Exercises

for "Scottish Bells"

1. *Downstrokes*

sim.

legato

(palm mute) *

2. *Alternate picking*

sim.

legato

3. *Variations (apply to #1)*

etc. (continue the pattern by ear)

4.

etc.

5. *More possibilities*

6.

7.

* for use in measure 7, beat 3 of "Scottish Bells"
  (and elsewhere)

The Story of the Rest

rest-stroke melody

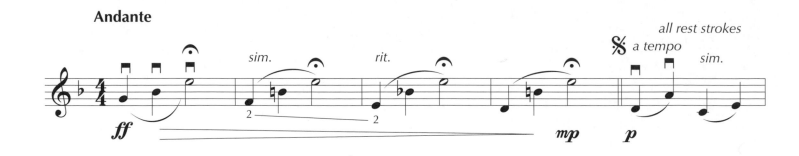

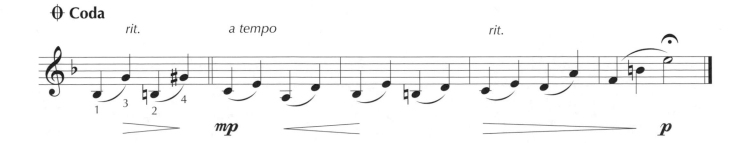

Exercises
for "The Story of the Rest"

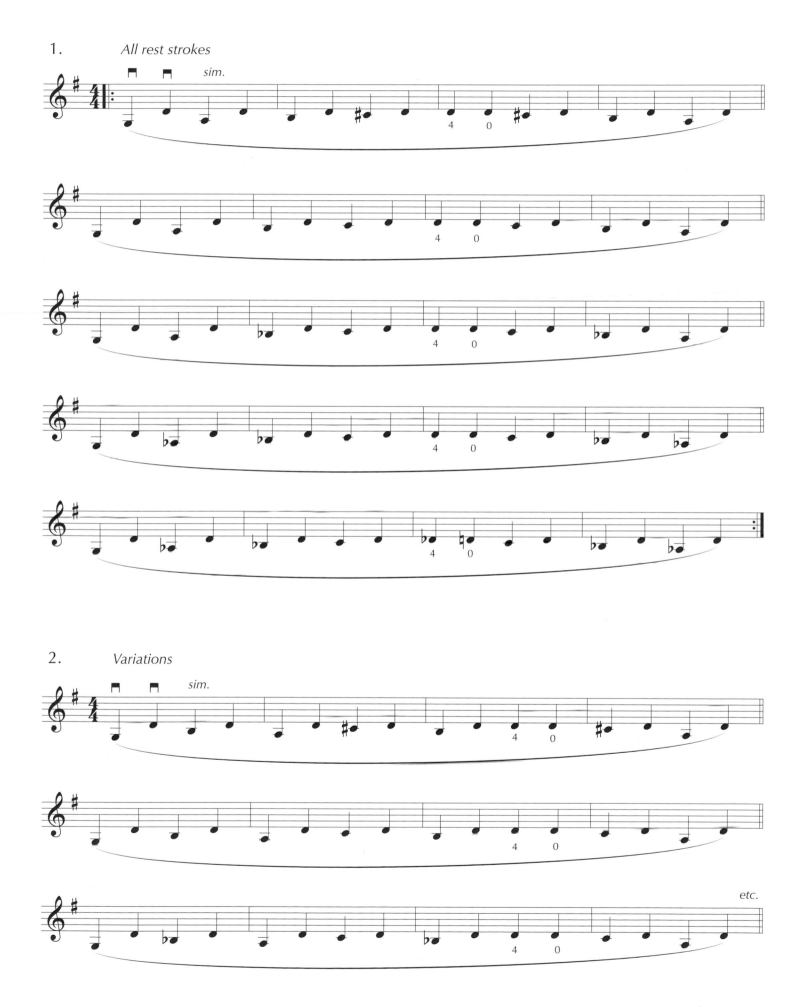

Exercises for "The Story of the Rest" (continued)

Road to Inverness

consecutive downstrokes, alternate picking, and optional glide strokes

Exercises

for "Road to Inverness"

8. *D major arpeggio pattern*

9. *C major arpeggio pattern*

second position

10. *B♭ major arpeggio pattern*

11. *Arpeggiated chord progression: D–C–B♭*

12. *Special fingering legato exercise*

Johann and Jethro

consecutive downstrokes, alternate picking, and optional glide strokes

Exercises

for "Johann and Jethro"

1. *Mixolydian scale pattern with two leaps*

2. *Half-step approach from below*

3. *Eight-note pattern with half-step approach from below*

4. *Alternate picking with two consecutive upstrokes*

5.

6. *Another arpeggio pattern*

Development 1
downstrokes, rest strokes, and alternate picking

Development 1 (continued)

Arpeggio Study 1

Chord Study 1
major triads, closed position

1. *Memorize chord shapes.*

2. *I–IV–I–V7 Chord progression with voice leading*

3. *Apply picking pattern to #2.*

4. *"Ode to Joy"*

Eighteenth-Century Mandolin Methods

Michel Corrette, 1772

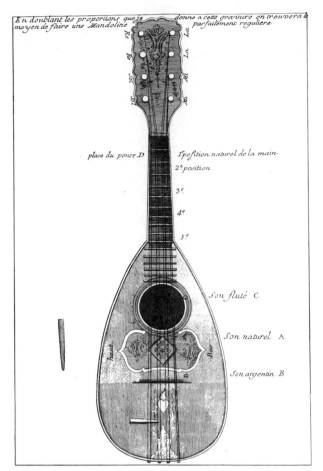

Gabriele Leone, 1768

Pietro Denis, 1768

Gabriele Leone, 1768

Part II: Reverse Alternate Picking

The Backward Thing

Part 1

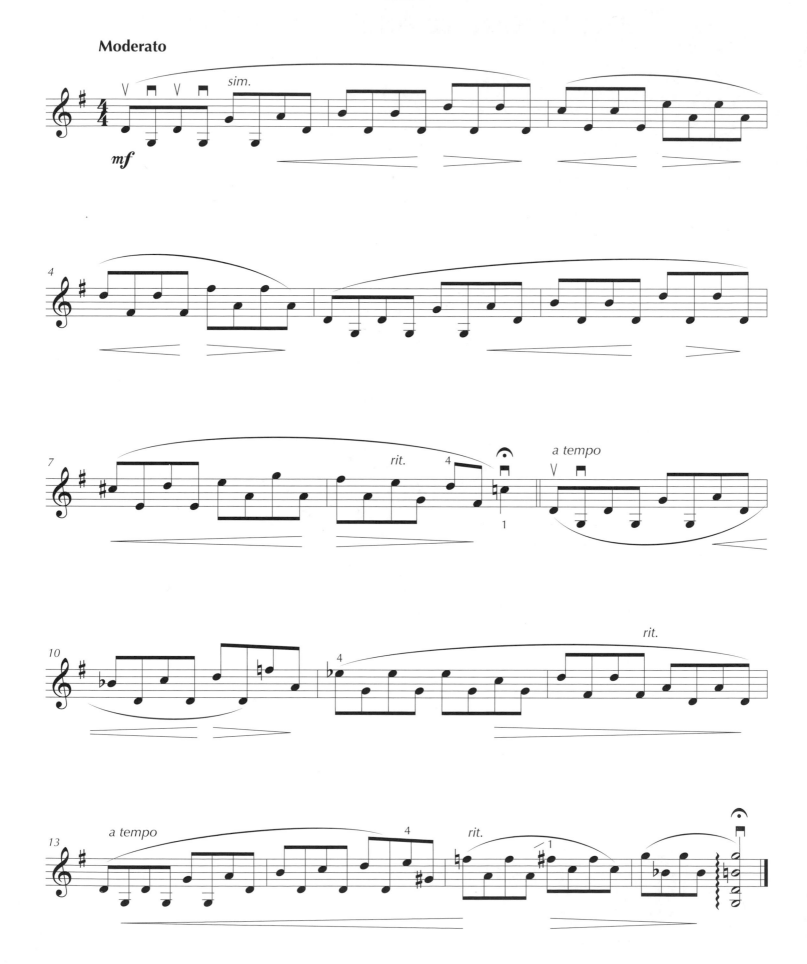

Exercises

for "The Backward Thing," Part 1

1. *Scale plus open string*

2. *Left-hand stretching exercise*

3. *G major scale in sixths and broken sixths*

4. *Accompaniment for "The Backward Thing," Part 1*

5. *Picking variations (apply to #4)*

6.

7.

The Backward Thing

Part 2

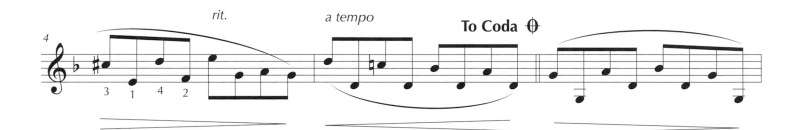

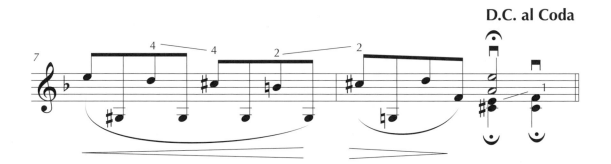

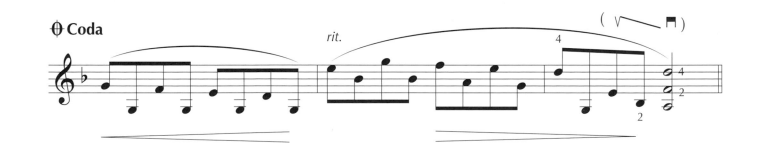

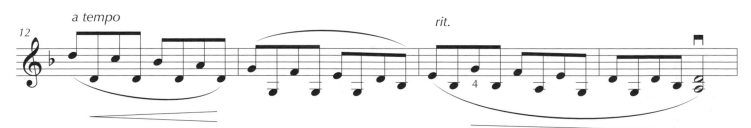

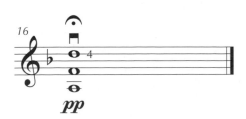

Exercises

for "The Backward Thing," Part 2

The Backward Thing
Part 3

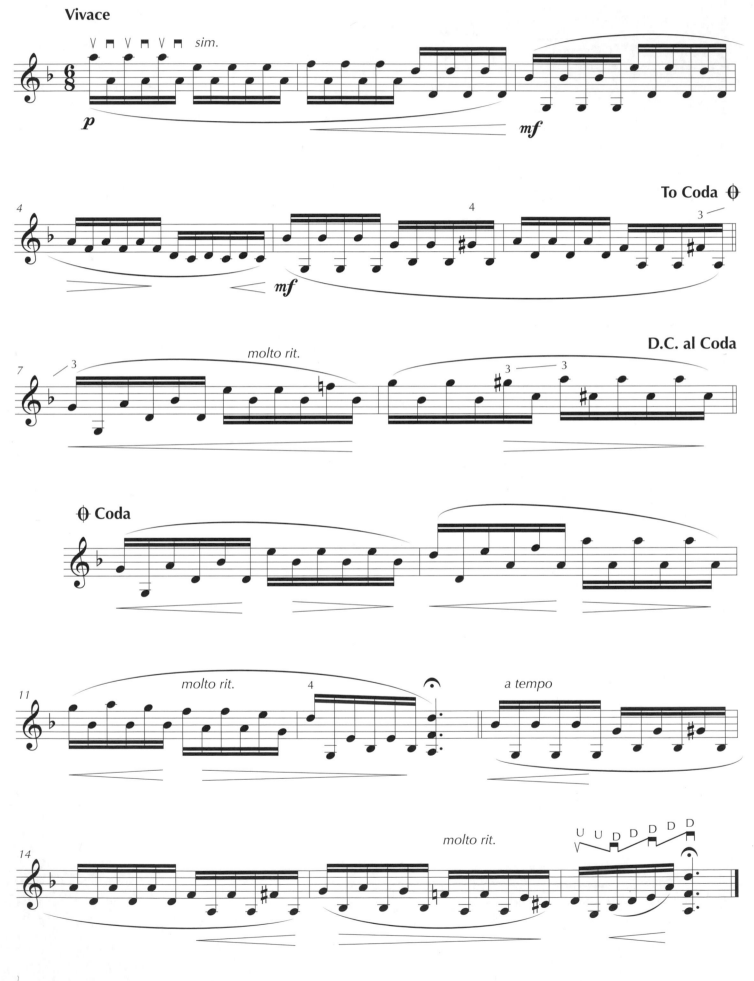

The Backward Thing
Part 4

Development 2

1. *Arpeggio shapes; memorize.*

5. *Provide inversions for 4i, 4j, and 4k.*

6. *Transpose the scale patterns (by ear) to closely related keys (A major, G major, D minor, C major, etc.).*

Arpeggio Study 2
the I–V7 progression, with voice leading

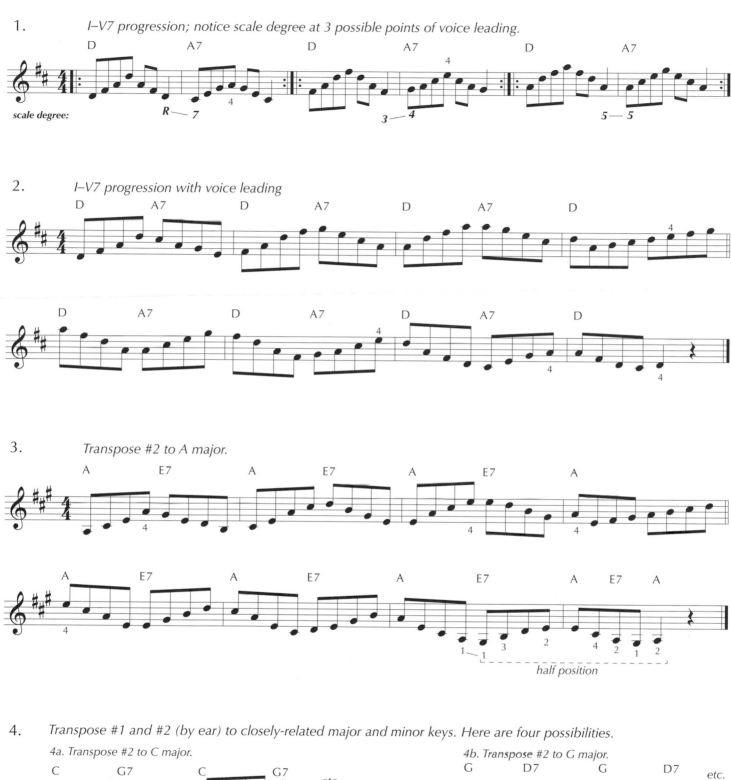

1.   *I–V7 progression; notice scale degree at 3 possible points of voice leading.*

scale degree: R — 7   3 — 4   5 — 5

2.   *I–V7 progression with voice leading*

3.   *Transpose #2 to A major.*

half position

4.   *Transpose #1 and #2 (by ear) to closely-related major and minor keys. Here are four possibilities.*

4a. *Transpose #2 to C major.*

4b. *Transpose #2 to G major.*

4c. *Transpose #1 to D harmonic minor.*

4d. *Transpose #2 to D harmonic minor.*

Chord Study 2
minor chords

1.   *Memorize chord shapes (Im–IVm–V7).*

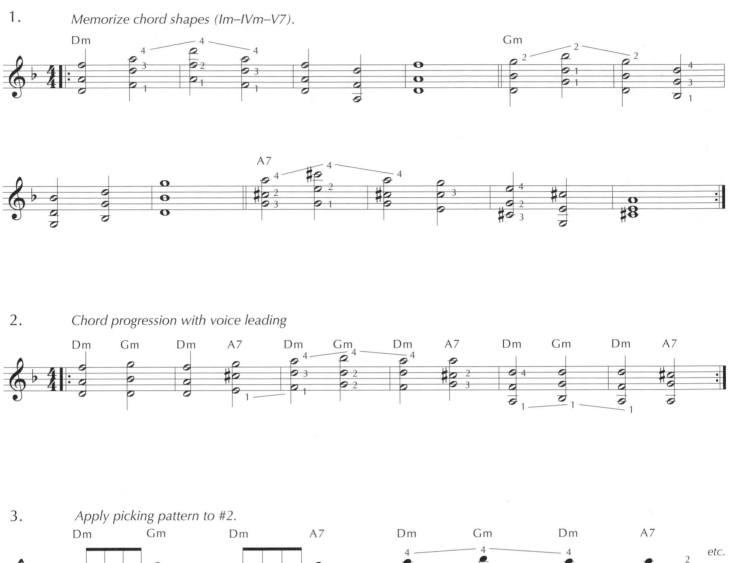

2.   *Chord progression with voice leading*

3.   *Apply picking pattern to #2.*

4.   *"Go Down Moses"*

Part III: Glide Strokes

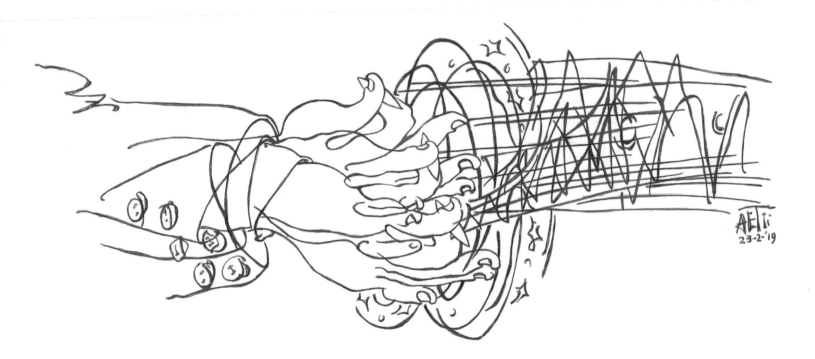

Downglide

Pick down-down-up throughout

Andante

Exercises
for "Downglide"

1.

2. *Double-stop arpeggios (open position)*

3. *Double-stop arpeggios (closed position)*

4. *Double-stop arpeggios (open and closed positions)*

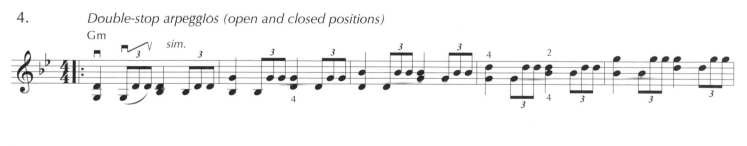

Upglide
pick up-up-down throughout

Adagio

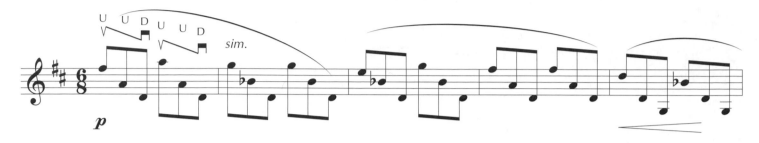

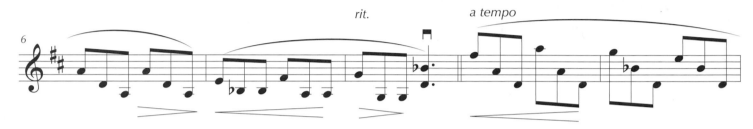

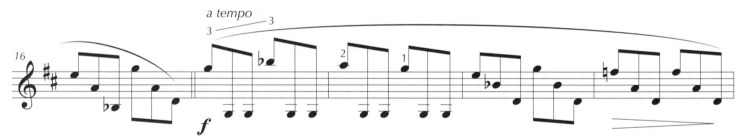

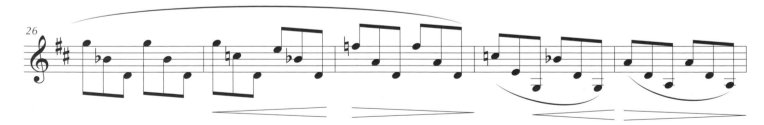

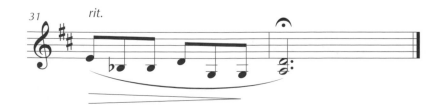

Exercises

for "Upglide"

1.
U–U–D on two courses

2.
Transpose #1 to these keys.

3.
U–U–D on three courses

4.
Wider reaches

5.
"Meditation on a Small Star"

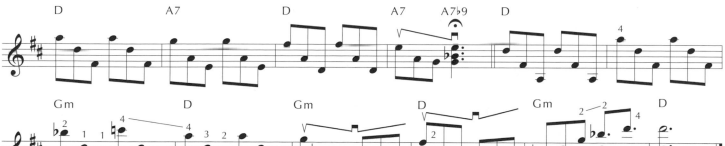

Forward and Reverse

Exercises

for "Forward and Reverse"

1. *D minor scale plus open string*

2. *Scale exercise: double-stop thirds and sixths*

3. *Chord shapes in G major; review.*

4. *Chord progression: I–IVm–V7–I*

5. *D–D–U across three courses*

Gliding Home

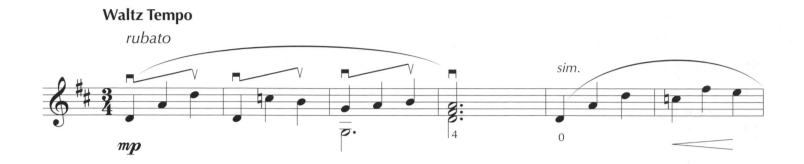

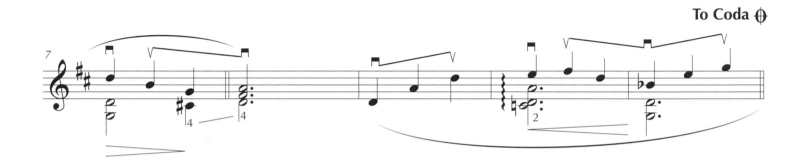

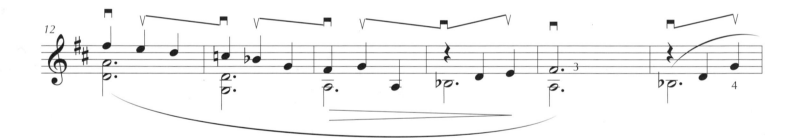

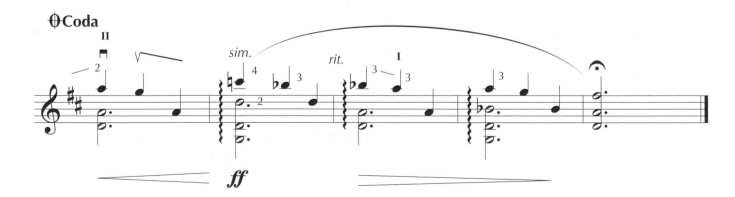

Exercises
for "Gliding Home"

1.

2. *Arpeggio studies: G minor*

3.

4.

5. *Arpeggio studies on "Gliding Home"*

D   D7   G   D   Gm   D   Gm   D

6.

D   D7   G   D   Gm   D   Gm   D

7.

D   D7   G   D   Gm   D   Gm   D

8.

D   D7   G   D   Gm   D   Gm   D

9.

D   D7   G   D   Gm   D   Gm   D

Development 3

glide strokes, reverse alternate picking, and double stops

Development 3 (continued)

Development 3 (continued)

9. *Pick direction and fingering study*

Arpeggio Study 3
voice leading the I–IV and I–IV–V7 progressions

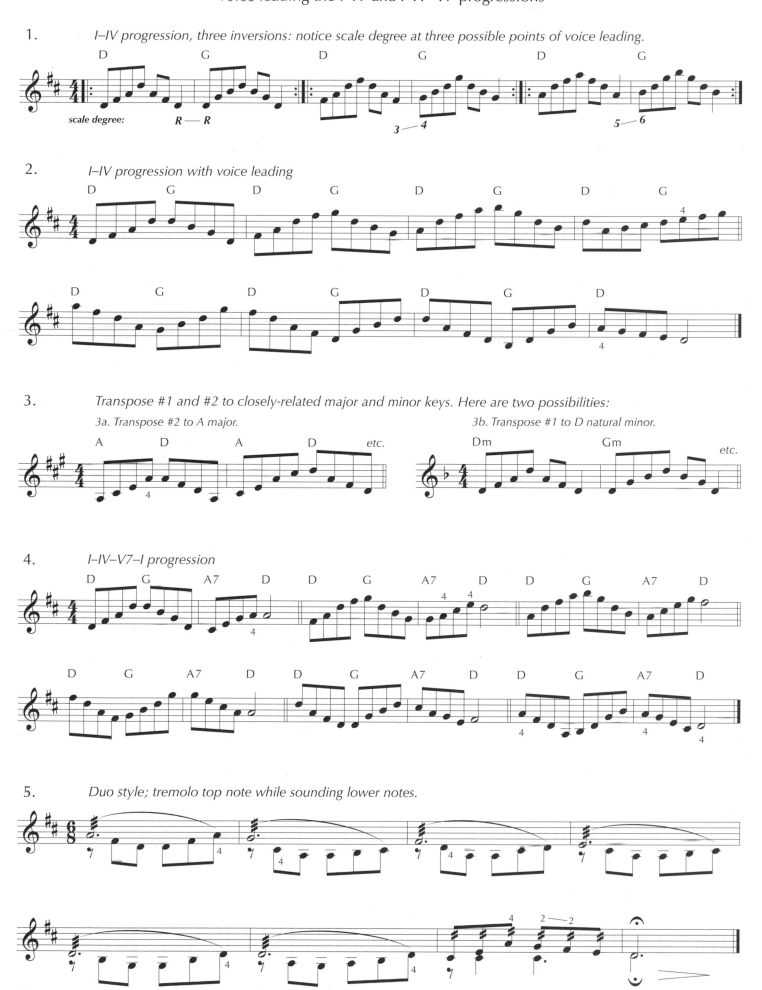

1. *I–IV progression, three inversions: notice scale degree at three possible points of voice leading.*

scale degree: R — R   3 — 4   5 — 6

2. *I–IV progression with voice leading*

3. *Transpose #1 and #2 to closely-related major and minor keys. Here are two possibilities:*

3a. *Transpose #2 to A major.*

3b. *Transpose #1 to D natural minor.*

4. *I–IV–V7–I progression*

5. *Duo style; tremolo top note while sounding lower notes.*

Chord Study 3
closed position

Part IV: Mixed Techniques

Old Joe Carr

Exercises

for "Old Joe Carr"

The Stalking of the Muse

Exercises
for "Stalking of the Muse"

1.

Closed-position arpeggios played on two courses; notice voice leading through I–IV–I–V progression.

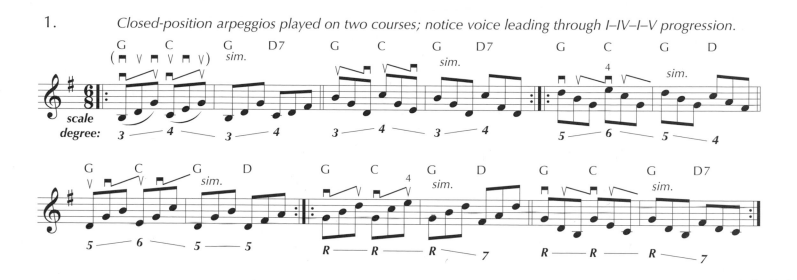

2.

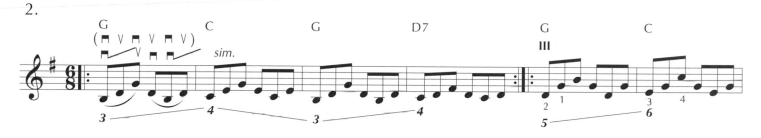

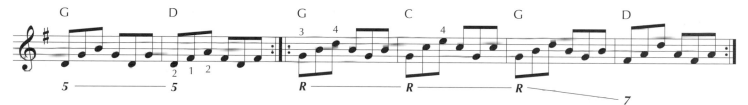

3.   *Arpeggio Etude*

For Kabalevsky

Exercises
"For Kabalevsky"

1. *Sixths*

legato

2. *Variations*

3.

4.

5.

6. *Duo exercise*

* flatten index finger
** flatten second finger

Morning in Our Town

Exercises

for "Morning in Our Town"

Carolan's Remorse

Exercises
for "Carolan's Remorse"

1.   *Chord voicings: key of D minor*

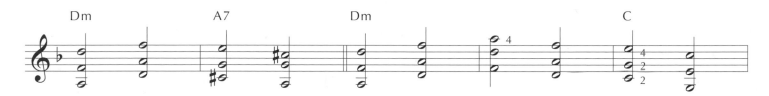

2.   *Variation*

3.   *"Scarborough Fair"*

Development 4

1.   *Arpeggios in third position*

2.   *Arpeggio exercises in first, second, and third positions*

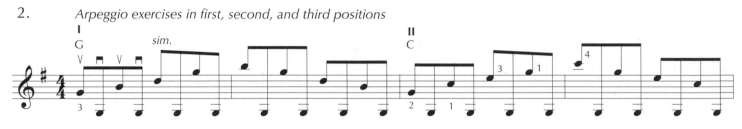

3.

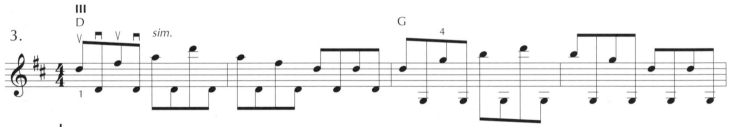

4.   *"Ode to Joy"*

52

Arpeggio Study 4

1. *Major scales harmonized with arpeggios*

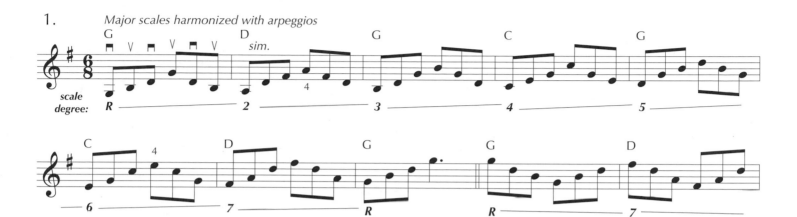

2.

3. *"Skater's Waltz" (Waldteufel)*

Chord Study 4
"Carolan's Draught"

Turlough O'Carolan

Moderato

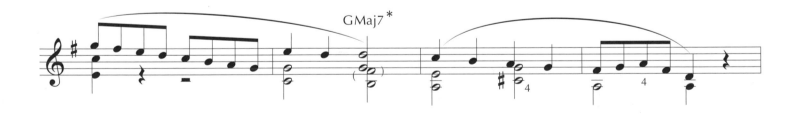

GMaj7 *

* optional split string voicing

Part V: Summary Etudes

Arpeggio Duo 2 plus 1

Duo #1

Allegretto

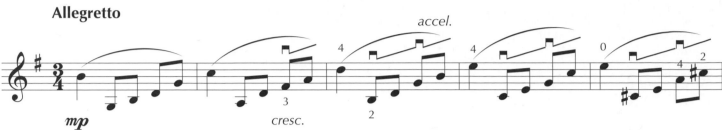

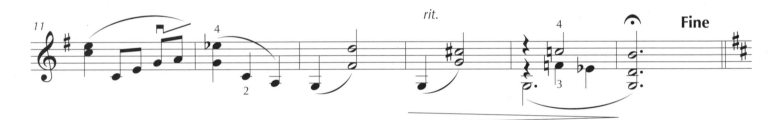

Duo #2

* prepare fingering on beat 1
   suggested order: Duos #1–2–1–3–2–1

Arpeggio Duo 3

The Big Glide

Summer's End

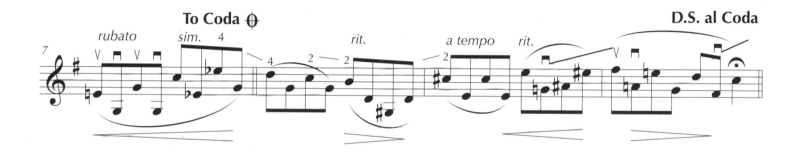

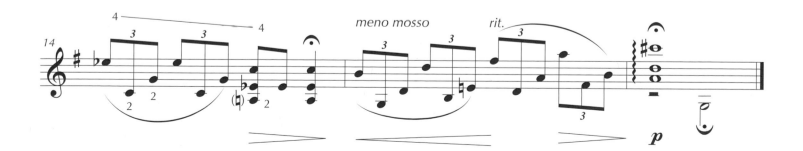

Tito's Lament

Adagio

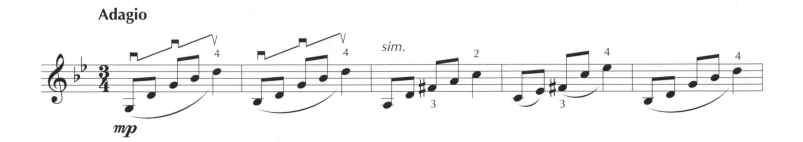

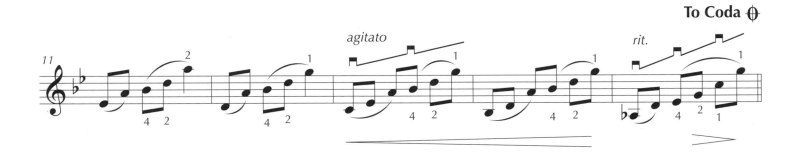

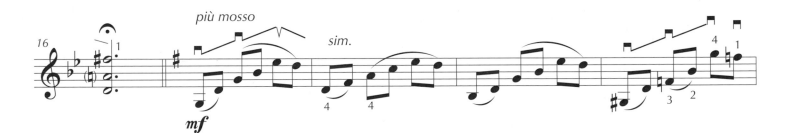

⊕ Coda

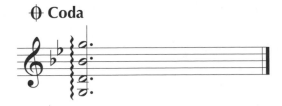

Waiting for Renzo

APPENDIX I:
The Reading Game
Notes from an Ear Training Teacher

"Reading standard notation." It sounds straightforward, no? Yet there are several different skills involved, and unfortunately it is possible to learn some while neglecting others. Here is how I think about the steps involved in learning to read music:

1. Recognizing the notes by name;
2. Associating those notes with the instrumental technique used to produce them;
3. Perceiving the distance in pitch between each note and the next;
4. Mentally "hearing" each note before it sounds;
5. Building intuitive ear-to-finger connections.

Note Recognition
The first step is recognizing the pitch of the written note by its position on the musical staff. Most people find it easier to learn several notes at a time, for example by constructing a diatonic, seven-note scale. Imagine meeting seven new people, each with different personalities: you can spend time getting to know them, but remembering them is easier… if you know their names!

"The F is on the E string, first fret"
At some point, reading standard notation on an instrument requires us to memorize the location of each note (on the mandolin fingerboard), or to otherwise memorize the technique used to produce each note. Indeed, many music students have learned this way: "Here's a C, play the C, Here's a D. . ." There's a time for this sort of blunt-force approach, but the problem is that many students somehow never get past this stage, to associate the visual stimulus of the written note with its sound. Some may continue for years without ever realizing that they have associated the written note only with the technique used to produce it. The sound of the note is a byproduct of this process.

Intervals
To get past the eye-to-finger habit, moving toward a more ear-centered approach, it is helpful to recognize the intervallic distances between notes. Perhaps that is why many classical mandolin methods begin with interval practice, moving up and down a diatonic scale by seconds (adjacent notes), followed by leaps of increasing intervals: thirds, fourths, and so on. In the process we learn to visualize any diatonic interval, beginning on any finger, without having to think of the next note's name. We also build a mental map of the fingerboard that helps to diagram the available notes in terms of diatonic intervals and their chromatic alterations. Once fluent in the process of reading diatonic intervals, it becomes much easier to read different clefs, or even (with practice, perhaps) to transpose on the fly.

I have often taught the concept of reading different clefs to a class of new ear training students by asking: "who has read alto clef?" (The usual answer: no one!) To students struggling with treble clef (and knowing they will have to learn the notes all over again in bass clef), the thought of having to learn more clefs, with the notes again in different locations, can be intimidating! But by having them sing a simple diatonic scale in treble clef and then moving the same scale to alto clef, the student is forced to rely not on naming the notes (whose locations are not yet memorized in the unfamiliar clef), but instead on reading intervals (up and down the scale, and then larger distances). In a very short time, the students understand that reading intervallically does not require us to think of the note names. It is a different process than reading the notes, and an entirely different thought process which can be used to navigate the fingerboard regardless of clef.

Audiation

Mentally "hearing" any desired note is something that people with perfect pitch are able to do—without context. Someone with perfect pitch is usually able to sing a pitch correctly simply by reading it on the staff, or the converse: to recognize and name a note being heard. For the rest of us, audiation is a process of comparing what we are hearing to something we previously heard: the notes we hear are understood through the context of a previously established key.

The first four notes of Beethoven's fifth symphony are not enough to establish a sense of tonality (identifying the key you're in), but as the melody continues, the ear tends to organize melody notes around a perceived key center. At this point, a person with well-developed relative pitch can work backwards to recognize those opening notes as the fifth and third degrees of the key (C minor: G – G – G – Eb). Over time, you may even begin to memorize pitches by their texture and develop a sort of partial "perfect pitch." Just now, while writing this example, I suddenly "heard" those first four notes of Beethoven V in my ear and was confident I was hearing them in the correct key. I had to check a recording to be certain, but I was indeed hearing G-G-G-Eb (only 10 more notes to perfect pitch!).

The advantage of well-developed relative pitch, when reading a new, unfamiliar piece from the page, is that it presents yet another point of reference. That reference depends on the ear retaining a sense of tonality that has previously been established. Once you perceive the key, all other notes can be analyzed and mentally "heard" in relation to it. In that split second before you play a note from the page, your ear envisions the pitch—so that hearing your instrument produce the note confirms what your ear has already "heard."

The Ear-to-Finger Connection

Once the audiation process is solid, seeing a written note enables us to hear that note mentally, even before the instrument sounds. The next step is building intuitive ear-to-finger connections based on familiarity with the fingerboard. By now we have reversed the process in step 2, where the sound was a byproduct of the technique. In this final step, the technique has become a spontaneous byproduct of the sound! It is essentially the same process we cultivate for improvisation. Beginning improvisers and readers both rely heavily on visual relationships to navigate the instrument (although this is more difficult on some instruments than others—try trombone!). Over time, we cultivate ear-to-finger connections, and instead of leading the process, technique gradually comes to occupy a more intuitive place in the process.

To summarize this discussion of sight-reading tools: First, we recognize and name the notes by their position on the staff; Second, we relate those notes to their locations on the fingerboard; Third, we build both ear and fingerboard skills by perceiving the distance from each diatonic note to the next (along with chromatic alterations); Fourth, we build the ability to mentally envision a pitch in relation to a pre-established key; Finally, all of these skills combine to build intuitive connections between ear and finger. The written note becomes the stimulus that sets the ear-to-finger connection in motion.

For classical mandolin, the ability to read written notation is an entry-level skill. Yet somehow, our culture sometimes sends the message that reading musical notation is difficult or only for specialists. We also tend to assume that purely aural traditions are more accessible, or closer to authentic "folk" culture. That's usually true, but in the mandolin world, the threads of classical and folk traditions are so entwined as to make those distinctions seem less important.

Some point to the centuries-old practice of tablature associated with early instruments such as lute or mandore, but I know of no performance tradition connecting those examples to mandolin. On the contrary, almost all written mandolin music (until recent years) has been written in standard notation. Music reading skills open the doors to these resources, plus a trove of music waiting to be adapted from other instruments. That's why as a teacher, I try to convey the message: Standard notation is easy, fun, and empowering!

APPENDIX II:
An 18th-Century Mandolin Lesson
Gabriele Leone: Arpeggiated chord voicings and chord melody

Every age has its own masters, and yet not every masterful achievement is remembered by the next generation. Perhaps that's one reason why, when studying the works of earlier times, we sometimes discover fresh ideas that seem outside of today's mainstream.

Much of the music in Gabriele Leone's 1768 method book is built on elaborate picking patterns that rely on specific combinations of downstrokes, upstrokes, and glide strokes. Leone illustrates these patterns and encourages us that, once memorized, the patterns may be freely substituted. In this way can create an improvisational approach useful for embellishing a solo piece or accompanying another instrument.

One charming feature of Leone's method is his way of arpeggiating three-note chord voicings. He begins by suggesting several ways to arpeggiate a basic C major triad on the bottom three courses:

For practice, Leone provides this chord progression:

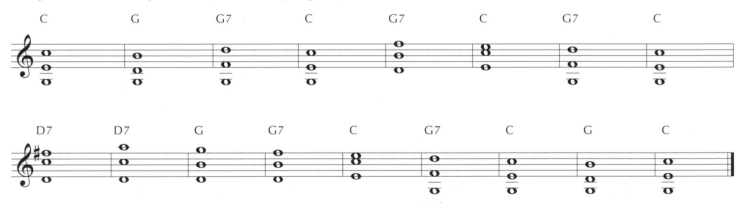

Each chord in the progression above has four beats, so you can apply the four picking patterns by repeating each once, to make a complete 4/4 measure. As you learn more picking patterns, Leone suggests extracting one or two beats from any pattern, and mixing to make new combinations.

Applying patterns #1 and #3 to Leone's chord progression would sound something like these two excerpts:

Now consider the elegant way Leone's chords connect: the top note of each chord connects to the next, to form a melody. As you play through the progression, stay focused on the top note:

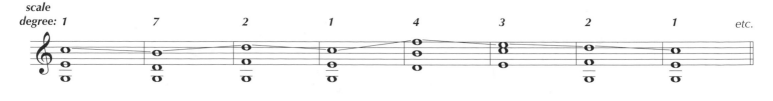

In essence, Leone has created a chord-melody by arranging chord tones below each melody note to form a chord progression. Not all the chords are complete; some are missing chord tones (even the third!) since the emphasis is on smooth resolutions and comfortable fingerings. In other musical styles we often change chords by moving the same voicing around the mandolin neck. In contrast, Leone's chords create an efficient, keyboard-like sound emphasizing linear motion and smooth voice leading.

Now, try applying Leone's chord progression to more of Leone's picking patterns:

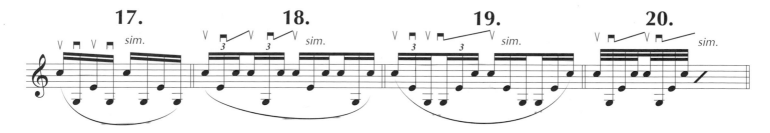

APPENDIX III:
THE ITALIAN MANDOLIN:
its evolution, nomenclature and types

by
Alex Timmerman

circa   1650   1680   1730

1 Mandola or **Mandolla**

1.

Italy. From c.1650 to c.1760.
3x2+1 or 4x2+1 strings of lamb gut.
Played mainly fingerstyle.
Tuned in fourths:
bb-ee-aa-d
gg-bbe'e'-a'a'-d''

2. Mandolino

Italy. From c.1670 to c.1800. 4, 5 and 6 double gut strings. Played fingerstyle and after c.1765 also with a plectrum made from the wood of the cherry tree.
Tuned in fourths:
3x2+1 strings = e'e'–a'a'–d''–g''(g'')
4x2+1 = bb-e'e'-a'a'-d''-g''(g'')
6x2 = gg-bb-e'e'-a'a'-d''-g''-g''

3. Chitarra Battuta

Italy. From c.1715 onwards. Played fingerstyle or with a feather quill. Of great importance for the development of the metal-strung mandolin types. Especially with regard to the inner construction: an upwards bent soundboard to withstand the downwards pressure of the metal strings.

8. Colascioncino
(a tre corde)

Italy. From c.1650 to c.1770. 2 or 3 single gut strings. Played finger style or with a plectrum made of the wood of the cherry tree.
Tuned in fifths of fourths.

9. Mandolino 'a quattro corde singole'

Italy. From c.1710 to c.1800. 4 single gut strings. Played with a plectrum made of the wood of the cherry tree.
Tuned in fifths: g-d'-e''

1. Mandola or Mandolla 3x2+1 gut strings c.1650 Venezia, Anonymous
2a. Mandolino 3x2+1 gut strings 1680 Cremona, Antonio Stradivari
2b. Mandolino 3x2+1 gut strings 1690 Perugia, Pietro A. Gavelli
2c. Mandolino 5x2 gut strings 1702 Perugia, Pietro A. Gavelli
2d. Mandolino 6x2 gut strings 1726 Roma, Benedetto Sanbretto
2e. Mandolino 6x2 gut strings 1797 Milano, Giuseppe Presbler
3. Chitarra battuta (5/6) 7x2 metal strings c.1750 Central Italy, Anon.
4a. Mandolino Genovese 6x2 metal strings c.1755 Genova, Cristiano Nonemacher
4b. Mandolino Siciliano 4x3 metal strings c.1760 Sicilia, Anon.
5a. Mandolino Napolitano 4x2 metal strings 1759 Napoli, Cavaliero Bonifacio
5b. Mandolino Napolitano 4x2 metal strings 1771 Napoli, Donatus Filano
5c. Mandolino Napolitano 4x2 metal strings 1790 Napoli, Giovanni B. Fabricatore
5d. Mandolino Napolitano 4x2 metal strings 1829 Napoli, Pasquale Vinaccia
6a. Mandolino Romano 4x2 metal strings c.1750 Roma, Anon.
6b. Mandolino Romano 4x2 metal strings c.1755 Roma, Gaspare Ferrari
6c. Mandolino Romano 4x2 metal strings c.1750 Roma, Anon (G. Ferrari)
7a. Mandolino Milanese or Torino 6x1 gut strings c.1795 Milano, Anon.
7b. Mandolino Milanese or Torino 6x1 gut strings c.1825 Milano, Anon.
8. Colascioncino Southern Italy (2 or) 3x1 gut strings c. 1655 Southern Italy, Anon.
9a. Mandolino 'a quattro corde singole' 4x1 gut strings c. 1700 Venezia, Anon.
9b. Mandolino 'a quattro corde singole' 4x1 gut strings 1761 Brescia, Carlo Sauli
10a. Mandolino Cremonese or Bresciano 4x1 gut strings c.1795 Cremona, Anon.
10b. Mandolino Cremonese or Bresciano 4x1 gut strings 1799 Cremona, Matteo Scolari
11a. Mandolino Napolitano moderno 4x2 steel strings 1891 Napoli, Gaetano Vinaccia
11b. Mandolino Napolitano moderno 4x2 steel strings 1900 Napoli, Raffaele Calace
11c. Mandolino Napolitano moderno 4x2 steel strings 1910 Napoli, Raffaele Calace
11d. Mandolino Napolitano moderno 4x2 steel strings 1921 Napoli, Raffaele Calace
12a. Mandolino Romano moderno 4x2 steel strings 1888 Roma, Giovanni de Santis
12b. Mandolino Romano moderno 4x2 steel strings 1865 Roma, Antonio Petroni
12c. Mandolino Romano moderno 4x2 steel strings 1899 Roma, Giovanni B. Maldura
12d. Mandolino Romano moderno 4x2 steel strings 1897 Roma, Giovanni de Santis
12e. Mandolino Romano moderno 4x2 steel strings 1905 Roma, Luigi Embergher
12f. Mandolino Romano moderno 4x2 steel strings 1927 Roma, Luigi Embergher
13a. Mandolino Lombardo or Milanese 6x1 gut strings c.1900 Milano, Carlo Albertini
13b. Mandolino Lombardo or Milanese 6x1 gut strings c.1900 Milano, [P. Armanini]
14. Mandolino Toscano 4x1 gut strings c.1900 Milano, Carlo Albertini

1.
2a.
2b.
2c.
2d.
2e.
3.
4a.
4b.
5a.
5b.
5c.
5d.
6a.
6b.
6c.
7a.
7b.
8.
9a.
9b.
10a.
10b.
11a.
11b.
11c.
11d.
12a.
12b.
12c.
12d.
12e.
12f.
13a.
13b.
14.

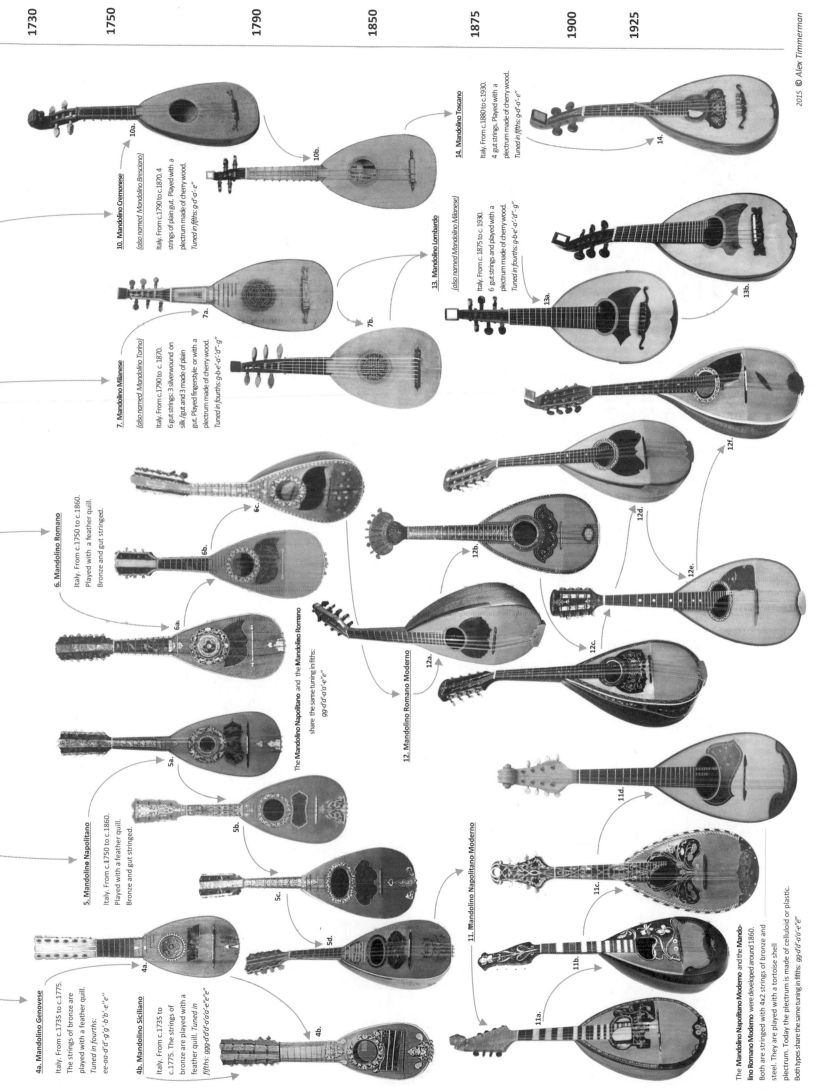

1730   1750   1790   1850   1875   1900   1925

2015 © Alex Timmerman

10. Mandolino Cremonese

(also named Mandolino Bresciano)

Italy. From c.1790 to c.1870. 4 strings of plain gut. Played with a plectrum made of cherry wood. *Tuned in fifths: g-d'-a'-e''*

14. Mandolino Toscano

Italy. From c.1880 to c.1930. 4 gut strings. Played with a plectrum made of cherry wood. *Tuned in fifths: g-d'-a'-e''*

7. Mandolino Milanese

(also named Mandolino Torino)

Italy. From c.1790 to c.1870. 6 gut strings: 3 silverwound on silk/gut and 3 made of plain gut. Played fingerstyle or with a plectrum made of cherry wood. *Tuned in fourths: g-b-e'-a'-d''-g''*

13. Mandolino Lombardo

(also named Mandolino Milanese)

Italy. From c. 1875 to c. 1930. 6 gut strings and played with a plectrum made of cherry wood. *Tuned in fourths: g-b-e'-a'-d''-g''*

6. Mandolino Romano

Italy. From c.1750 to c.1860. Played with a feather quill. Bronze and gut stringed.

The **Mandolino Napolitano** and the **Mandolino Romano** share the same tuning in fifths: *gg-d'd'-a'a'-e''e''*

12. Mandolino Romano Moderno

5. Mandolino Napolitano

Italy. From c.1750 to c.1860. Played with a feather quill. Bronze and gut stringed.

11. Mandolino Napolitano Moderno

4a. Mandolino Genovese

Italy. From c.1735 to c.1775. The strings of bronze are played with a feather quill. *Tuned in fourths: ee-aa-d'd'-g'g'-b'b'-e''e''*

4b. Mandolino Siciliano

Italy. From c.1735 to c.1775. The strings of bronze are played with a feather quill. *Tuned in fifths: ggg-d'd'd'-a'a'a'-e''e''e''*

The **Mandolino Napolitano Moderno** and the **Mandolino Romano Moderno** were developed around 1860. Both are stringed with 4x2 strings of bronze and steel. They are played with a tortoise shell plectrum. Today the plectrum is made of celluloid or plastic. Both types share the same tuning in fifths: *gg-d'd'-a'a'-e''e''*

67

About the Illustrator

Alex Timmerman's "fast and filmic" pen drawings, often featuring musicians, have a distinctively recognizable style. They have appeared on CD booklets, concert posters, and music magazines throughout the world. Alex's illustrations for books and paintings are many, and his paintings are on permanent exhibition at 'De Galerie' in Amsterdam's P.C. Hooftstraat. He has also exhibited in art galleries in Ängelholm and Malmö, Sweden, and painted for private clients.

Raised in a Dutch family where the visual arts were greatly appreciated, it was obvious that, like two of his brothers and his sister, young Alex would also find his way to the art academy. Alex studied to become a goldsmith, but soon changed his studies to classical guitar at the ArtEZ Conservatory in Zwolle.

In the music world, Alex is best-known for his significant contributions as a musicologist, teacher, instrumentalist, and conductor. He has lectured on the subject of plucked instruments at universities, music high schools, and conferences. One such presentation to the European Guitar and Mandolin Association (Trossingen, Germany, 2004) sums up work of great significance to the international mandolin community: *"The Roman mandolin; its development and perfection by Luigi Embergher."* Alex has documented the work of Roman luthiers active from the end of the 17th century through the completion of the modern Roman Mandolin around 1900.

As a teacher and conductor, Alex has made important contributions by applying knowledge gained from his historical research. Alex uses the Roman mandolin technique (with its elongated, double-pointed plectrum), documented in Silvio Ranieri's *"L'Art de la mandoline."* Toward the end of the twentieth century, the Roman approach had been nearly forgotten. Alex began to teach the Roman technique to a new generation of Dutch students, continuing this unique chapter of mandolin history. Some of Alex's students, including Sebastiaan de Grebber and Ferdinand Binnendijk, are among a new generation of Roman-style mandolin virtuosos.

Alex is also founder and conductor of the mandolin-guitar ensemble Het Consort, the platform through which his musical vision has been expressed. In more than 20 years of performing, the ensemble has participated in many international collaborations, and premiered many original works composed for mandolin chamber orchestra. The members of Het Consort, amateur and professional alike, devote their free time with great enthusiasm and dedication to create a community orchestra of the highest artistic level. All plectrum instruments are modern Roman mandolins made by Luigi Embergher and his direct successors, Domenico and Giannino Cerrone, Pasquale Pecoraro, and Lorenzo Lippi.

In 2019, Alex was appointed to the Honorary Board of Directors of the Classical Mandolin Society of America.

About the Author

photo by John McClain

August Watters is a multi-stylistic mandolinist, composer/arranger, conductor, and teacher who is deeply involved in today's revival of this elegant instrument; and has made significant contributions to the recovery and advancement of its traditions. His work as an interpreter, improviser, composer, and arranger bridges contemporary classical music, jazz, folk music traditions, bluegrass, and the historical concert mandolin repertoire.

Originally from Texas, August grew up in a rich musical environment with strong connections to both classical and American folk music. His father was an opera singer, classical radio host, and choral director; his mother is a church organist, general music teacher, and librarian. During his teen years, August absorbed the rich bluegrass music culture of southern Indiana, living near Bill Monroe's music festival in Bean Blossom, Indiana. He studied jazz with David Baker at Indiana University, and moved to the California bay area in 1981 to join the "new acoustic" scene beginning to flourish around David Grisman, Darol Anger, Mike Marshall, and others. It was there that he discovered Rudy Cippola, a direct link to America's early mandolin orchestra tradition. August went on to study at Boston's Berklee College of Music, where he focused on composing for both large and small jazz ensembles. After graduation, August spent ten years in the commercial music industry working primarily as an arranger/orchestrator/conductor for other composers, and producing underscore and theme music for The Monitor Channel, PBS, and others. During this era he contributed several string jazz quartet arrangements that were included for years in the Berklee String Department curriculum.

August taught at Berklee College of Music for 18 years (1998-2016), where he earned the rank of Professor of Ear Training. He also founded and taught a bluegrass/jazz "Acoustic String Project" ensemble for fifteen years (2000-2015), and taught String Department labs and private mandolin lessons. As a clinician he has lectured and performed widely in Europe and the USA on the American mandolin and its roots in Italian folk and classical concert music traditions.

August's book *Exploring Classical Mandolin* (Berklee Press, 2015) is an internationally recognized resource for teaching and self-study. In 2019, excerpts were included in a graded list of repertoire recommended to mandolin teachers by the Australian and New Zealand Cultural Arts organization. August is also known for his original study resources for mandocello and mandola.

August holds a Master of Music in Music Education from Boston University, as well as a Bachelor of Music from Berklee College of Music, summa cum laude, majoring in Jazz Composition and Arranging. He is the founder of the New England Mandolin Ensemble and the Festival of Mandolin Chamber Music. August is also an Emmy Award-winning arranger, currently focused on original music for mandolin ensembles, new works for solo mandolin, and the early American mandolin repertoire.